Bird's-Eye View of the Pueblos

Taos, main section of the "North House" group.
Notice irregularity in roof levels.
Adobe construction.

Bird's-Eye View

of the Pueblos

By STANLEY A. STUBBS

Norman : University of Oklahoma Press

To Kenneth M. Chapman

Acknowledgments

My sincere appreciation and thanks to Miss Amelia E. White, who made this study possible, and to all others who helped— some in an unwitting capacity.

Aerial photographs were made by Cutter-Carr Flying Service, Albuquerque, New Mexico. The photograph of Taos Pueblo was furnished through the courtesy of the New Mexico Tourist Bureau.

Foreword

For many years the villages of the Pueblo Indians of Arizona and New Mexico have received comparatively scant attention, considering the innumerable studies that have been made of the ceremonies, customs, beliefs, and habits of the people living in them. They have been referred to sometimes in rather uncomplimentary terms as mere mud villages, or described in a very general way as communal structures, often multistoried, built around a central plaza. Inasmuch as they reflect the history, social structure, and religious system of the people, they are in themselves worthy of thorough study. It is important to record the actual ground plan of each one of them before time and cultural changes bring about their ultimate disappearance.

Almost all of the many reports on excavations of prehistoric sites in the Southwest include ground plans showing the arrangement of these ancient structures. But, with very few exceptions, we have no record of the ground plan of the pueblos still being occupied. Victor Mindeleff, in 1882–83 made an architectural study of the Zuñi and Hopi towns. For years this report stood as the only study of its kind.

In the early nineteen thirties, a project called "The Historical American Buildings Survey" was undertaken by the federal government. The mission churches at Ranchos de Taos and Laguna were completely recorded, and a full study of the pueblo of Acoma was made. These studies, covering hundreds of pages of drawings done in such detail that the buildings could be reconstructed from the plans, are an invaluable record. Plans for a similar study of Taos Pueblo were never carried out. Such a project to cover all of the pueblos would be most desirable, preferably under a long-term government program. In some instances, however, even the federal government would be balked by the reluctance of the Indians to permit any survey work within their villages.

Since such studies are lacking, and since it is impossible to map many of the pueblo villages from the ground, it was suggested that vertical aerial photographs be taken, and from these the plan of each village be prepared. These pictures were made, and they form the basis of the present study. The scale in each drawing is based on actual ground measurements taken on structures in each pueblo, within the view area. For ease in comparison, the ground plans are laid out so as to be in the same plane of view as the aerial photographs. Because an optical illusion may result if aerial photographs are not viewed from the proper angle—buildings becoming depressions and holes becoming mounds—"north" is not always at the top of the page as in conventional cartography. The fairly recent trend to build houses away from the communal center is made obvious by a comparison of the aerial view and the plan. None of the secondary towns built during the nineteenth and early part of the twentieth century are included in this study, for with few exceptions they do not follow the traditional pattern of pueblo layout, and are indistinguishable from the Spanish villages in the same region. These later constructions would logically comprise a separate study in themselves.

Among questions brought up at the inception of this study were: What, if any, is the Spanish influence on pueblo-planning? Is the layout dictated by traditional style? Only in the older villages—in all but the more recent portions of these—can answers to such questions be found. It is hoped that the evidence herein presented will serve as source material for others working in the field.

This report is not intended as an architectural study of each town, although the type of construction strongly influences the character of growth. Its purpose is primarily to record, by means of aerial photographs supplemented by ground plans showing details not visible from the air, the layout of the major villages as they were in 1948. In the ground plan of each pueblo, an attempt has been made to show as many of the room outlines as possible. In some cases, however, this can not be determined from the aerial view. Also, earth-covered porches look like completely walled rooms. These minor items, however, do not materially change the value of the plans.

From Spanish chronicles and early historical records, we know that certain villages were occupied when the first white men came into the area. In many cases, however, these records are not exact enough to actually locate a given pueblo, and to say that the present site is the one occupied by a town of that name in 1540. This is where the archaeologist assists the ethnologist and the historian. From time immemorial man has thrown his broken weapons and utensils, his trash and garbage, onto refuse heaps. Modern man has trucks to haul this accumulation away. Primitive man merely tossed it out around his habitation or a short distance away. The sequence of things used, eaten, or made by any group of people can be very clearly determined by a careful study of the refuse mounds. This holds true even with our own culture: the upper deposits of the city dump will yield evidence of radios, electric lights, automobiles, can openers, and razor blades; the lower levels will produce kerosene lamps, traces of the horse-and-buggy days, mustache cups, and fewer tin cans; even deeper, if the city has been occupied since Colonial times, there will be the objects brought to this country from their homeland by the English, French, or Spanish settlers. With the pueblo sites, prehistoric and modern, pottery is a major key to the sequence of development and length of occupation. Potsherds, the broken fragments of pottery discarded on the refuse mounds, are of great use to the archaeologist working in the pueblo region. He has found that the ceramic changes which have gone on here outline very clearly the time sequence, given in even more exact terms by means of the tree-ring chronology. Since man first began making pottery in this area, at about the same time as permanent habitations appeared, the craft has developed rapidly. A style was never static for long; each minor area and time period had, and still has, its distinctive ware. Pottery types are so thoroughly classified that we can say that a certain type belongs to a limited time horizon. If the pottery types, usually in the form of sherds, are found in appreciable quantities in a village site, we can be fairly certain of the time range of occupation of that site. Where excavation is not possible, as in the modern pueblos, we must depend on this method of dating.

The methods used in this study are a combination of archaeology and ethnology. The developing pattern of layout and architectural technique has been observed in hundreds of prehistoric pueblo sites, and is readily distinguished in the existing villages; the sequence of pottery types which can be picked up on the refuse heaps of ancient and contemporary villages is established. This part is archaeology. The language spoken, the ceremonial customs, the civil organization, and the present economy of contemporary pueblos are facts known through ethnology. All branches of anthropology are important in a complete understanding of the Pueblo Indian. Herein is presented primarily one facet of this understanding—a recorded pattern of the layout of the major existing Pueblo villages. Since the anthropology of the Southwest has always emphasized other phases of the subject, the main discussion deals principally with the development of building practice and pattern, disregarding to a large extent the material and abstract manifestations of Pueblo culture. The reader interested in general archaeology and ethnology in their broader phases is referred to the Bibliography.

Since spellings of the names of some of the pueblos have not yet become standardized, it has been necessary to choose among the variants. The spelling of the Hopi town names is that used by Fred Eggan, University of Chicago, in personal correspondence. The native names given for each pueblo are taken from *Days in the Painted Desert and the San Francisco Mountains,* by Harold S. Colton and Frank C. Baxter; *Ethnogeography of the Tewa Indians,* by John P. Harrington; and *Handbook of American Indians,* edited by Frederick Webb Hodge.

The population figures quoted, except those for the Hopi villages, are the 1948 census figures provided by the Indian Service. Hopi population data from the same source are shown below: Polacca, Hano, Sichomovi, and Walpi, listed together as "First Mesa," 1,285; Mishongnovi, 298; Shipaulovi, 152; Shongopovi, 423; Sunlight Mission, 61; New Oraibi, 590; Old Oraibi, 199; Hotevilla, 644; Bakavi, 176; and Moenkopi, 640. Because no figures are given for individual First Mesa towns, it being almost impossible to obtain an accurate census of each Hopi village, the 1932 figures listed by Colton and Baxter are used for all the Hopi towns and probably still represent fairly accurately the number of people actually living in the old sections of each town.

STANLEY A. STUBBS

Santa Fé
September 5, 1950

Contents

Bird's-Eye View of the Pueblos

By Way of Introduction

The Southwest, using the archaeologist's definition, is that portion of the country extending from western Texas to western Arizona as far as the Colorado River, and from southern Colorado and Utah down into northern Mexico. It comprises the region occupied during the last fifteen hundred years by pottery-making, agricultural, village-dwelling Indians.

Many people traveling along the highways of the Southwest have their first and only contact with living Indians—not the feathered version seen in western motion pictures, but sellers of curios and trinkets in roadside stands. However, one cannot judge their culture by this minor economic contact.

Before going any further, let us interpolate an explanation of the term "Pueblo culture." Man's primary needs are food, clothing, and shelter. With these provided, he begins to look around for frills and labor-saving devices. If his food problem is more or less answered, he has more time to devote to other endeavors such as ornamentation, social organization, and religion. The introduction of agriculture—the tools, techniques, and crops—into the Southwest was the foundation for Pueblo development. A good crop assured the major food supply for the coming year, but, once planted, required that the people stay close to their fields, to care for, and protect it from other groups. This necessity for a fixed abode developed the building practices, at the same time allowing leisure for the development of the

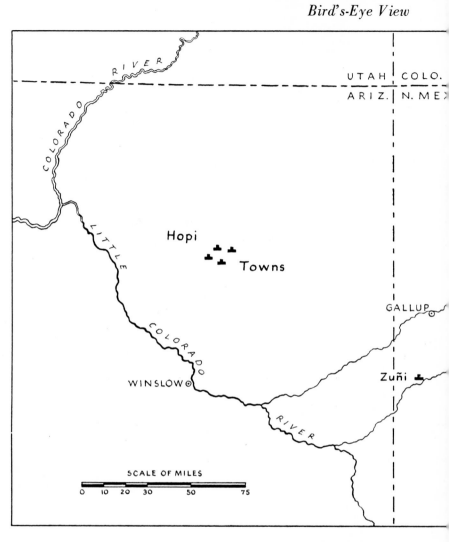

The Pueblos of

the Southwest

sedentary arts by the release of the people from constant food–gathering and hunting. However, agriculture in a semiarid country poses its own problems. Except in the higher elevations of the Southwest, the country is semiarid to arid. The region was, and in many areas still is, in a precarious balance between almost enough water and drought conditions. Crops—chiefly corn, beans, and squash—were produced in most parts by dry farming or floodwater irrigation. Under these conditions, water meant life to the people. Therefore, almost all ceremonies developed around the prayer for rain and efforts to keep their many supernatural deities favorable towards them. It was this environment and the necessity for unified action that produced the Pueblo culture and the unique villages indigenous to this part of the world.

Basically the Pueblo Indian is, and has been for generations, a farmer. In recent years he has added the raising of livestock, principally sheep and cattle, to his activities. The main crops, depending somewhat on the location of the pueblo, are the native corn, beans, and squash, with plants introduced by Europeans—wheat, oats, alfalfa, chili, melons, grapes, apples, plums, peaches, and apricots—becoming more and more important.

The craft industries of pottery, weaving, basketry, jewelry-making and leatherwork, most of which have been carried over from prehistoric times, originally served the need of the individual for his own use or for trade. In early times, pottery, shells, turquoise, textiles, and skins were widely traded. With the advent of the white trader, the Indian's economy still remained largely a form of trade and credit. Only recently has the Indian begun to use cash as the basis of his economy instead of the old subsistence form. An appreciable part of this income is derived from the sale of handicraft products. Certain villages are well known for their pottery, others for baskets or silverwork. In general, pottery-making has been reduced to the manufacture of objects such as ash trays, small jars, and knickknacks small enough for the traveling public to carry easily. The making of utility pieces such as water containers, cooking pots, and food bowls is almost a thing of the past. It is much easier and more practical for the Indian to purchase the dishes and utensils offered in the white man's store. Unless a craft has a commercial outlet or a personal practical use, it will vanish. The Indian will produce only those things which he can sell, and the low quality of most of the objects for sale today in the roadside stands and curio stores is a commentary on the poor taste of the tourist.

The term "communal living" has been applied to the Pueblo Indians' mode of existence, but in the strict sense this use is erroneous. The reservation lands apportioned to each group under the early Spanish land grants, later confirmed by the United States, and land added to these holdings by various means, chiefly range and grazing land, are communally held; the houses and farm land can be owned by an individual, family, clan, or community. However, this ownership of real estate is under informal community control. In general, individual ownership of real and private property, with exchange, trade, and sale undeterred by village authority, is increasing.

Each pueblo, excepting the Hopi towns, is controlled in itself by a governor, annually elected, who has charge of the secular affairs of the village. He is assisted by a lieutenant governor, a council, and special officers, such as the official town chauffeur. Since the Hopi escaped the full domination of the Spanish from 1680 to 1850, they hold closer to the probable prehistoric pattern of government, in which a hereditary chief or clan head has the informal control or guidance and is the village chief for life. In the New Mexico pueblos, the governor and his council form the pueblo court, which has jurisdiction over all conduct except crimes such as rape, murder, and arson, which are tried in the federal courts.

Religious control within the pueblo or moiety is under the cacique, who holds lifelong tenure, and who is assisted by society heads and other officials. Most pueblos are divided into two moieties, usually referred to as the "Summer People" and the "Winter People," or the "Squash" and the "Turquoise." Each moiety conducts the ceremonies pertaining to its half of the year. Usually each moiety has its own kiva, and unless political factions have split the unity of the village, most dances are held in the central plaza. The larger number of kivas in Acoma, Zuñi, and the Hopi towns is due to the custom of each clan or fraternity maintaining its own meeting place. The winter dances still held by the Pueblo Indians are in many instances hunting ceremonies —prayers for abundant game and success in its capture. The spring, summer, and early fall ceremonies are for fertility, rain, and harvest, and have developed as a result of the agricultural economy.

The Pueblo Indians of the Southwest all have very similar customs, beliefs, and economy, but are divided into several dialect and linguistic groups. So different are the languages spoken by the various tribes that a Pueblo Indian from Taos, for example, must use either English or Spanish when talking with a Pueblo from Santo Domingo. The main linguistic groups are:

Tanoan:
　　Tiwa: Taos, Picurís, Sandía, Isleta
　　Tewa: San Juan, Santa Clara, San Ildefonso, Nambé,
　　　　Tesuque, Hano
　　Towa: Jémez
Keresan:
　　Eastern: Cochití, Santo Domingo, San Felipe, Santa
　　　　Ana, Zía
　　Western: Laguna, Acoma
Zuñian:
　　Zuñi
Uto-Aztecan (Shoshonean):
　　Hopi villages (except Hano)

Man was living in this region sometime not long after the close of the last Ice Age, but all we know definitely is that he

8

was here and made easily identifiable stone implements with which to hunt now extinct animals. He left no traces of any habitation; probably he took advantage of caves and rock shelters, or possibly crude brush structures built in the open. It was not until after the beginning of the Christian Era that man began to use the materials around him to fashion more or less permanent dwellings of which we can find evidence today. Environment has always exerted a strong influence upon man's creative ability; he has used and developed those things which he found around him and made the best of what he had. Man in the semiarid Southwest developed a style of building adapted to the materials available, the climate, social conditions, and for defense from other groups.

About A.D. 300, the first of these crude attempts at architecture by the Indians living in the northern part of the Southwest began to appear. There were various types: the pit house, a dwelling in whole or in part subterranean, fashioned by digging a pit of the desired shape in the earth and either roofing the pit over directly or building up walls of stone, adobe, or wood to support the roof; the jacal, also called "wattle and daub," a shelter made of upright poles and brush, often plastered with adobe; and "wood and mud masonry," an early style of surface building in which short logs and sticks were used in place of stone and held together with adobe. These were only large enough to be single-family dwelling units, but were usually clustered in an irregular pattern forming a village. As time went on, these early inhabitants began to build small structures of masonry above the ground to serve as storage rooms. Such rooms were gradually enlarged to be used as living rooms; these in turn took on a more compact arrangement, as well as additional rooms, to become the small pueblo, or unit house, capable of housing several families.

Then, for some reason, an urban urge resulted in the building of the great terraced communal structures covering many

9

acres. It was these large villages that the Spanish explorers in 1540 first saw, and called by the Spanish name *pueblo,* or "village," in contrast to the temporary settlements of nomadic Indians.

Many of these villages, both large and small, ancient and modern, are located on high mesas or points of land which would aid in the defense of the village in case of attack. Sites in the open very often show a defensive layout, with rooms built entirely around a central court or plaza, or with only narrow passageways leading into the plazas. This defensive development of building has led to much speculation. Some have claimed it was due to the increasing raids of nomadic groups pushing into the Southwest, while a few advance the idea that the supposedly peaceful Pueblo Indians were actually quite aggressive and always in trouble with their blood neighbors over water rights, land claims, and religious and secular disputes. Much the same condition existed during the period of the city-states in Europe, when each town was a unit unto itself and against every other.

While the Pueblo Indians are considered a sedentary group, it must be realized that during their long occupation of the region, they have moved around a great deal. Village locations have been shifted constantly because of disasters such as fire and floods, because of the advantage offered by more favorable farming locations or better defensive sites, and also because of factional splits within a single pueblo. The great number of prehistoric sites in the Southwest can in large measure be accounted for by these recurrent removals, rather than an enormous population during pre-Columbian times. Between 1300 and 1540, however, there was a great reduction in the area occupied by Pueblo Indians. The Pueblo Revolt of 1680, when all the Spanish colonists were driven from the Pueblo area, and the Reconquest of 1693 brought about many shifts of population and changes of village location. Some of these were due to the desire of the Spanish to concentrate the Indians in fewer villages in order to maintain closer military control and also to aid in converting them to Christianity. The Indians, on their part, notably the Hopi, sought locations easier to defend, in fear of retribution from the Spanish. They still occupy many of these sites. However, even those villages founded after 1693, and before 1800, still follow the traditional plans developed by long generations of pueblo builders.

If the present-day Pueblo Indian culture pattern be projected back in time, disregarding fairly recent breakdowns of the old conservative ideas, one may get some idea of the need for large, consolidated towns. With the communal form of life closely controlled by the interlocking religious beliefs and secular customs, it was essential for control, as well as for protection, to keep all members of the group in close and rather confined contact. A similar trend is noticeable in our own culture. The early, generally rural, form gave way to the development of large urban centers; everyone wanted to get away from the farm, to get into the city to enjoy better wages and an easier way of life. Now, with improved transportation, people are beginning to move out from the great cities into suburban districts. The concern of the Indian is not for personal advancement and easy living, but rather for conscious integration and participation with the group in its ceremonial striving for supernatural assistance in gaining a living in a harsh environment, and for the mutual protection of numbers. With the breakdown of the ceremonial life, the adoption of the white man's ways, and the lack of necessity for unit defense, the Indian village has begun to break up; individual families build their homes away from the congested traditional center and form scattered suburban-type communities around the old village. The development and decline of the ground-plan pattern of the pueblos can be traced step by step from the earliest known structures in the Southwest up to the present day, not alone on typological grounds, but also by the evidence supplied by stratification, ceramic and other material culture traits, and by actual dates supplied by the tree-ring chronology.

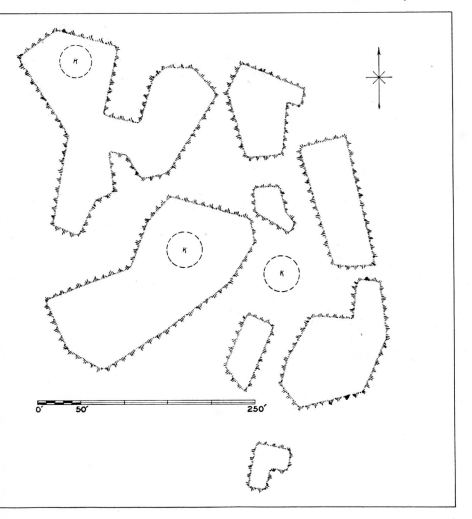

FIGURE 1. Irregular layout of prehistoric site. Located at the junction of the Rito de la Olla and the Río Grande del Rancho, about seven miles south of Taos. Main period of occupation: thirteenth century. Compare this pattern with that of the modern pueblo of Taos. Kiva location shown by circles. Laboratory of Anthropology Site 260.

12

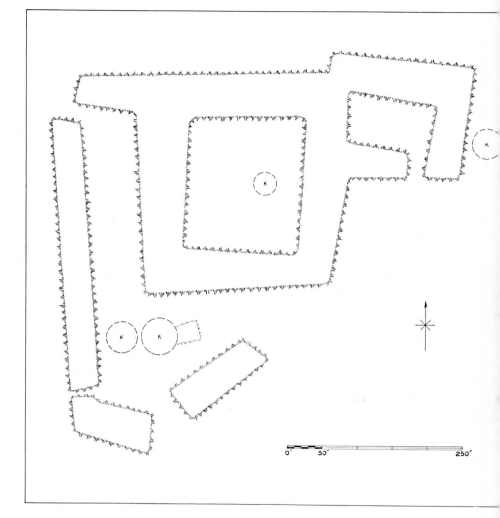

FIGURE 2.   Plaza layout of prehistoric site. Located on the west bank of Ojo Caliente Creek, about one and one-half miles above Ojo Caliente, north central New Mexico. Main period of occupation: fourteenth century. Kiva locations shown by circles. This site has been called Hupobi (Harrington, Twenty-ninth *Annual Report*, B.A.E., p. 161). Laboratory of Anthropology Site 380.

13

The style of architecture and the methods of building have largely determined the layout of a pueblo. Three main patterns are noticeable in pueblo plans. First: an indiscriminate clustering of house groups in one limited area. There may be one or more plazas, all very irregular, house blocks not following any definite alignment. (See Fig. 1, Rito de la Olla.) Second: more or less regular building around a central plaza or plazas. (See Figs. 2 and 3, Hupobi and Homolobi No. 2.) Third: rows of parallel house blocks with the space between forming streets which serve the same purpose as the plazas—a place to hold the dances. This street arrangement is a parallel design and is in no way related to the checkerboard layout of European and American towns. Few examples of the parallel-street layout exist in prehistoric villages, but both Acoma and Oraibi can be taken as type sites for this style, since they date back long before any European influence.

Kubler, in his recent study of the sixteenth century Mexican architecture, gives a good outline of Spanish town-planning of that period. The cross street or checkerboard is basic, and there is usually a central square with the church at the east end. Since most of the Pueblo Indians, especially in the Río Grande area, are nominally Catholic, the church is usually a prominent structure in the village. But only in one pueblo, Isleta, is it the central feature around which the town has grown. Even here the streets follow no regular pattern, but wander at random among the houses. In the other pueblos the church occupies whatever space was available, perhaps on the plaza, as in Tesuque, or at some distance from the center of the town, as in Santo Domingo.

Of even greater importance than the church in the life of the pueblo is the kiva. This is the ceremonial chamber which serves as the center of the Indians' own religious practices and ceremonies. The name is of Hopi origin. Kivas are of two forms, circular and rectangular; they may be subterranean, semisubterranean, completely above ground, or incorporated within the

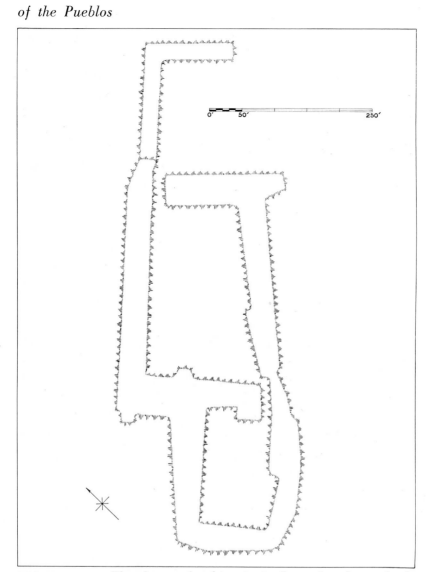

FIGURE 3.   Plaza layout of prehistoric site. Located on the east bank
of the Little Colorado River, about nine miles below Winslow, Arizona.
Main period of occupation: thirteenth and fourteenth centuries. This
site has been called Homolobi No. 2 by Fewkes (Twenty-second *Annual
Report*, Part 1, B.A.E., p. 29). Laboratory of Anthropology Site 420.
Compare with modern Hopi villages, especially Shipaulovi.

15

house blocks. Detached, rectangular kivas are characteristic of the Hopi villages; rectangular kivas are situated in the house blocks at Acoma and Zuñi; circular kivas are predominant in the Río Grande pueblos, although the rectangular type is found in a number of these towns.

The central plaza serves as the common center of both the Spanish town and the Indian pueblo, but the plaza idea in each culture is of independent origin. The single and multiple plaza arrangements occur in numberless prehistoric pueblo examples throughout the Southwest. Modifications and blendings of these types are also common in both early and recent times.

In the semiarid Southwest, wood as a building medium was not readily available to the Indian, and even when it was obtainable, he did not have proper tools for its shaping. He did, however, have unlimited amounts of stone and adobe, that common calcareous, sandy clay so plentiful in this region, having good plastic qualities, and drying to a hard, uniform mass. The adobe was, and still is, used as a mortar for the stone masonry or used alone for building entire walls. Before the introduction by the Spanish of the making of form-shaped, sun-dried bricks, which marks an important change in the building methods but not in the architecture, the Indian built up his walls in layers, patting each new course of adobe onto the dried mass below and extending it to such height as his plastic material would allow, until the wall reached the desired height (Plate 1). Walls of this construction can still be seen in the older portions of those villages which have been occupied since before 1540. Where available, flat sandstone slabs were the preferred masonry medium because they were easy to lay up; although sometimes dressed square, they were more often only roughly broken to the needed size. Where sandstone was not obtainable, waterworn or irregularly shaped stones were laid up in an adobe mortar. This type of masonry is not so substantial as the other, but stands up surprisingly well if the wall is protected with a fresh coat of adobe plaster each year.

PLATE I.   Coursed adobe construction, in a prehistoric pueblo
(1250–1350) near Santa Fé, New Mexico.

17

Adobe walls must also be given an annual coating of mud plaster to protect them from the weather.

Whatever type of wall construction was used in a pueblo, following the aboriginal pattern, the first step was the digging of a shallow trench. This was filled with stone or adobe to serve as the foundation on which the wall was built. In the first layout of a pueblo, a number of adjoining rooms might be built simultaneously; to this unit core, rooms would be added by accretion. The final structure therefore took on an uneven outline, for each builder followed his own ideas of height and room size, dictated somewhat by tradition. With the addition of new stories, the irregularity of the roof line became more and more pronounced, as is especially apparent in the modern pueblo of Taos (frontispiece). In the "South House," the view from the north shows three stories; the south view of the same building shows four stories. Such conditions must be taken into account when studying the aerial views and plans.

Bonding of corners was not typical of pueblo masonry until fairly recent years; one wall was built up to another to form a room corner and held in place by adobe mortar and the weight of the wall. In coursed adobe construction, the corners were generally well tied together by the courses running completely through the corner or turning and being common to two walls.

Roof construction was fairly consistent throughout the pueblo area. Logs or poles were laid across the short axis of the room; on this grid smaller poles, brush, reeds, or bark were laid and then topped with a layer of adobe, which served as the flat roof or, if upper stories were added, as the floor of the higher room.

In most early pueblo structures, roof construction accounted for most of the wood used in the main building. Brush-and-pole shelters, or arbors, which appear both in prehistoric and in modern villages, are secondary to the main pattern. Wooden doors and window frames are a European influence. In general, prehistoric buildings had no doorways at ground level; rooms were entered through hatchways in the roof. This was a defensive measure. Low doorways connected inner rooms or gave access from the lower roof levels to outer upper-story rooms. Windows were absent, except as small ventilating or smoke holes.

The introduction of the white man's building methods, both technique and placement, has modified to a certain extent the outside appearance of the older pueblos, and these methods have almost completely dominated those recently built. In the older towns this has been a gradual change, brought about through the necessity for repair and rebuilding of more ancient structures, or the intentional remodeling of rooms to conform to the newer style, chiefly by the addition of ground-floor doorways, glass windows, and larger rooms. Such changes are a part of the inevitable ac-culturation of the group, and so is the recent trend to build each home as a unit away from the central plaza area; but these changes have not altered the basic design of a pueblo built on the traditional layout. Other innovations, such as the pitched roof of tin, can be used in separate individual houses, but can-not be so easily adapted to a solid house block formed of indi-vidual rooms each having a different roof level.

It should be reiterated here, by way of summary, that the major Pueblo villages of the Southwest are laid out along lines dic-tated by patterns of building developed by generations of pueblo-builders. The reluctance of some of the present-day Pueblo In-dians to adopt the white man's ways, and the tenacity with which they cling to their own religion and customs are clearly reflected in the compact traditional layout of the village in which they live. Those villages which are occupied by less conservative, more acculturated, or more amalgamated people have broken further from the pattern, but unless the village is of quite recent date, the core of the town still says "Pueblo."

In any part of the country where moisture is excessive, this Pueblo type of architecture would not be satisfactory. But here it is eminently successful, as witness its long survival and its

19

adoption as the basis for modern Southwestern architecture. The "Santa Fé" or "Pueblo" stylized architecture of today, so well adapted to the region, is a direct descendant of the early pueblos whose developmental steps have been traced back for hundreds of years.

The Pueblos

Taos

Probably a Spanish variation of the native name Tua, meaning
house, houses, or village. (Harrington.)
Location: both sides of Taos Creek, about sixty-five miles north
of Santa Fé, New Mexico.
Linguistic group: Tiwa.
Period of occupation: present village, about 1700.
Construction: adobe, irregular plaza type.
Population (1948): 907.
Reservation: 47,334 acres.
Annual *fiesta:* September 30.

Because of its mountain setting and its spectacular high-terraced
houses, Taos has been visited, photographed, and painted probably more than any of the other pueblos. The village visited in
1540 by Alvarado is not the same as the present one, but the de-
scription given at that date still fits—"the houses are very close
together and have five or six stories." The old village was on both
sides of the river, as now, but to the north and east of its present

23

Taos

PLATE II

24

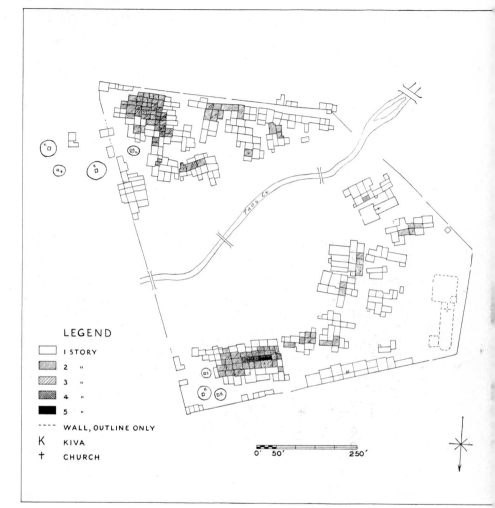

LEGEND

☐	I STORY
▨	2 "
▧	3 "
▨	4 "
■	5 "
----	WALL, OUTLINE ONLY
K	KIVA
+	CHURCH

0' 50'   250'

Taos

FIGURE 4

location. Traditional stories tell of the burning of the old town, probably in 1693 or 1694.

Of all the pueblos, Taos is the only one surrounded by a wall. The Taos Creek divides the town into what is called the North House (five stories high), and the South House (four stories). The old church, destroyed in 1847, and the newer edifice are situated in the western part of the walled area. While the section within the wall still presents the compact pattern of a traditional pueblo structure, many of the younger people are building individual homes in the adjoining fields. Seven circular, subterranean kivas, one of which is no longer used, are located in two groups along the eastern line of the pueblo. The broad roadway, parallel to the river at the east, is used for the ceremonial races. Covered passageways, a feature of Hopi towns, and at one time of Zuñi, appear only in Taos of all the Río Grande pueblos.

Craftwork at Taos has almost completely died out; no decorated pottery has been made for generations, the only production being a micaceous-ware cooking pot, quite similar to that made in Picurís. Some work in buckskin is carried on, mainly for domestic use.

Picurís

Also called San Lorenzo. According to Harrington, the name is derived from the Spanish Picurís, but Hodge says that it comes from the Keresan name, Pikuria.

Location: the north bank of the Río Pueblo, about twenty miles south of Taos, New Mexico.

Linguistic group: Tiwa.

Period of occupation: at least since 1200.

Construction: adobe, plaza type, both the old and the new sections.

Population (1948): 130.

Reservation: 14, 959 acres.

Annual *fiesta* and Summer Corn Dance: August 10.

The plaza portion of Picurís just west of the church is recent, though still exhibiting the ancient pattern of town-planning; the old section lies immediately to the north, and much of it is reduced to mounds covered with sherds, outlines and fragments of walls, and abandoned houses which now serve as corrals and stables. Like Oraibi, much of Picurís is now archaeology.

Taos and Picurís, on the northern frontier of the pueblo area, were subjected to greater contact with some of the Plains In-

Picurís

PLATE III

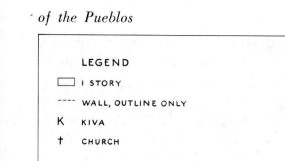

LEGEND

☐ I STORY

---- WALL, OUTLINE ONLY

K KIVA

† CHURCH

0' 50'   250'

Picurís

FIGURE 5

dians. Many of the present customs of dress and ceremony derive from these Indians rather than Pueblos, but even with this culture-borrowing, the homes retain the traditional pueblo pattern.

Picurís, like Taos, gave up the manufacture of painted pottery about the time of the Pueblo Revolt. Since then, it has specialized in a cooking ware characterized by a large amount of yellow mica in the clay, which gives the finished pieces a bronze, metallic look. This pottery has been widely traded among the Pueblos and the Mexicans, and even the Anglos, for it is said that beans taste better when cooked in one of these jars; the same idea as the "Boston bean pot" for baked beans.

Sandía

Spanish for "watermelon." The native name is Nafiat, "dusty" or "sandy" place. (Harrington.) Sandía is also the name of the mountains directly east of the pueblo.

Location: east side of the Río Grande, fourteen miles north of Albuquerque, New Mexico.

Linguistic group: Tiwa.

Period of occupation: Sherds found on the refuse mounds show a continuous series from about 1300 to the present.

Construction: adobe, plaza type, with modified parallel street layout.

Population (1948): 139.

Reservation: 22,884 acres.

Annual *fiesta* and Green Corn Dance: June 13.

Spanish chronicles indicate that Sandía was one of the pueblos of the Province of Tiguex (Tiwa) visited by Coronado in 1540. The old part of the village, now largely reduced to mounds and rows of foundation stones, is mainly between the church and the highway. Most of the inhabitants are reported to have fled to the Hopi country at the time of the Pueblo Rebellion of 1680, and remained there until 1742. The sherd evidence suggests no great gap in the occupancy of the site. The Hopi name for the village

31

Sandía

PLATE IV

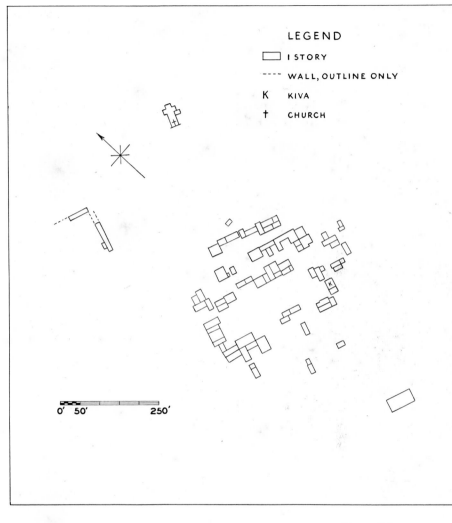

LEGEND

☐ 1 STORY

---- WALL, OUTLINE ONLY

K KIVA

† CHURCH

0′ 50′ 250′

Sandía

FIGURE 6

Sandía

is Payupki, which is also the name for a ruined pueblo located on the Second Hopi Mesa, built and occupied, according to tradition, by Indian refugees from the Río Grande area after the Pueblo Revolt. The kivas at Sandía are rectangular and are built into the house blocks.

No handicrafts are at present being followed. Such pieces of pottery of native manufacture as are used are obtained from Santo Domingo or Zía.

Isleta

Spanish for "little island." The native name is Tuei, meaning
"town." (Harrington.)
Location: west bank of the Río Grande, about thirteen miles south
of Albuquerque, New Mexico.
Linguistic group: Tiwa.
Period of occupation: The date of the founding is doubtful.
Construction: adobe, plaza type, with extreme scattering.
Population (1948): 1,470.
Reservation: 187,826 acres.
Annual *fiesta* and Harvest Dance: September 4.

In actual ground coverage, Isleta is the largest of the existing
pueblos. The population figure includes Isleta, Chicale (a village
on the east side of the river), and Oraibi. This last is the name
given to the small settlement just southwest of Isleta, founded
about 1880 by conservatives from Laguna who moved to the Río
Grande and joined Isleta after splitting with the progressive
faction at the old site. Whether Isleta occupies the same site as
the village of that name in 1540 is uncertain. No sherds found in

Isleta

PLATE V

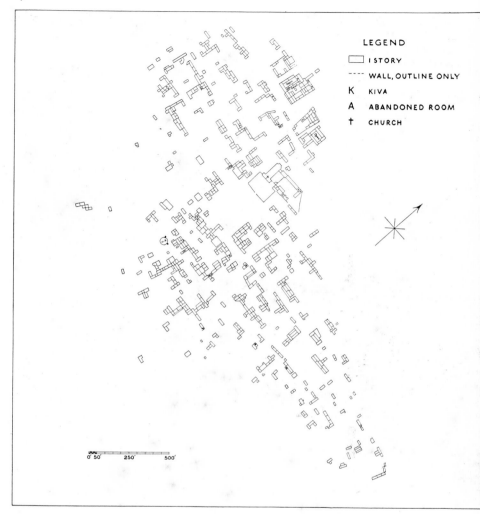

LEGEND
☐ I STORY
---- WALL, OUTLINE ONLY
K KIVA
A ABANDONED ROOM
† CHURCH

0' 50'   250'   500'

Isleta

FIGURE 7

the extensive refuse mounds indicate an earlier date. The name indicates location on an "island," which may have been the lava point now occupied, or a nearby situation which has been obliterated by floods or farming activity. From surface indications, it seems likely that a date early in the sixteenth century would fit the evidence. A church was built at some time before 1629. Since Isleta was refounded after the Reconquest, the present village can be said to date after that time. Intersecting streets in the village are the result of accident rather than deliberate planning. A single, circular kiva is located south of the plaza; if specialized rooms used as kivas exist within the house blocks, none have come to our attention. Isleta del Sur, just below El Paso, Texas, was founded in part, in 1681, by Indians from Isleta who had been captured by Otermín.

Like their Tiwa-speaking relatives to the north, the inhabitants of Isleta have made no painted pottery since about 1700. A plain red cooking ware has been made for domestic use, but the pottery called "Isleta" sold in curio stores and at the railroad station in Albuquerque is almost exclusively the product of the Laguna colony. This pottery is brick red in color with a white slip and black and red designs. Usually the vessels are in the form of small bowls.

San Juan

Spanish for St. John. The native name is Oke'onwi. (Harrington.)
Location: east bank of the Río Grande, about thirty miles north
    of Santa Fé, New Mexico.
Linguistic group: Tewa.
Period of occupation: since about 1300.
Construction: adobe, modified parallel-street type.
Population (1948): 768.
Reservation: 12,213 acres.
Annual *fiesta* and Corn Dance: June 24.

San Juan is bordered on two sides by the settlement of Chamita,
only a road separating the Tewa- and Spanish-speaking groups.
The consolidated pueblo layout is quite evident by a comparison
of the two parts of the community shown in the aerial photograph
(Plate VI). The two roads forming a cross in the center of the
picture divide San Juan from Chamita; the pueblo occupies the
upper left-hand quarter. The south half of Chamita is typical of
the European system of individual family house–spacing. The

39

San Juan

PLATE VI

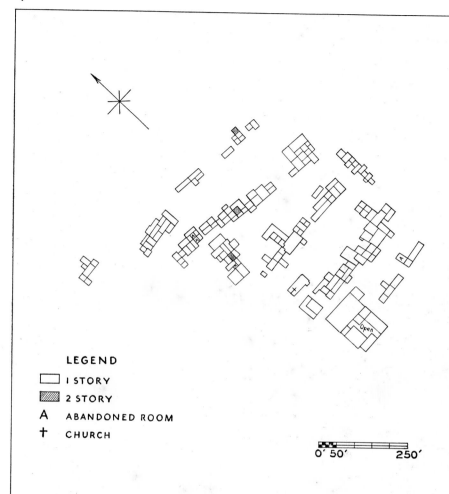

San Juan

FIGURE 8

LEGEND
☐ I STORY
▨ 2 STORY
A ABANDONED ROOM
✝ CHURCH

0' 50'   250'

main portion of San Juan consists of three long, irregular house groups, roughly parallel. The kivas are rectangular, and are enclosed in the house blocks. San Juan has a permanent farming suburb called New York.

In 1598, Oñate with his Spanish colonists established provincial headquarters across the river at San Gabriel, and because of the generosity of the San Juan Indians, gave their town the name San Juan de los Caballeros. Almost a century later, as a result of the severities and mistakes of the Spanish authorities, San Juan produced Popé, the instigator and leader of the Pueblo Revolt.

Plain, polished pottery, both red and black, has been for many years the standard product of San Juan potters. About 1930 a revival of an old style of decoration was started, consisting of incised, geometric line patterns, often overelaborated into intaglio patterns. Polychrome designs on polished red also appear.

Santa Clara

Spanish for St. Clare of Assisi. The native name is Kapo'onwi. (Harrington.)

Location: west bank of the Río Grande, two miles below Española, New Mexico.

Linguistic group: Tewa.

Period of occupation: probably founded in the fourteenth century.

Construction: adobe, plaza type, recent scattering.

Population (1948): 573.

Reservation: 45,742 acres.

Annual *fiesta* and dance: August 12.

Sherds collected at Santa Clara are not of sufficient number to allow an exact statement as to length of occupation. However, the pueblo was in existence for some time prior to the coming of the Spanish. The double quadrangle arrangement of two plazas noted by Bandelier in the eighteen eighties still exists, but sections of the older houses are falling into disrepair and the new building is away from the plazas. The kivas are rectangular, surface structures, distinct from the house blocks.

43

Santa Clara

PLATE VII

44

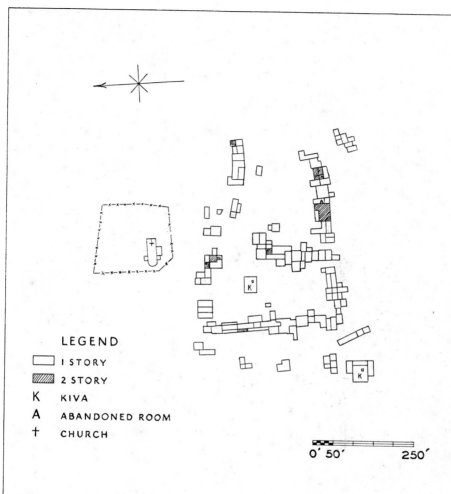

LEGEND
☐ I STORY
▨ 2 STORY
K KIVA
A ABANDONED ROOM
† CHURCH

0' 50'   250'

Santa Clara

FIGURE 9

Santa Clara

Santa Clara and San Ildefonso have felt the impact of the Atomic Age more than the other pueblos. Being situated close to Los Alamos, they have furnished many employees for that project. This source of relatively high income drastically influenced their economy.

During the summer season especially, when a car full of visitors drives into the plaza of Santa Clara and parks, it is almost immediately surrounded by a circle of women and girls, each with her basket of small pottery objects for sale. The pottery formerly made here was almost entirely polished black, somewhat like that of San Juan, and not so highly polished as that from San Ildefonso. Within the last fifteen years, a polychrome style, more closely resembling the pottery of San Juan, has been produced. However, the commonest pieces now seen for sale in the pueblo are the little animal figures of polished black pottery—horses, cows, pigs, alligators, skunks, and birds.

San Ildefonso

Spanish for St. Ildefonsus. The native name is Poqwoge'onwi,
"pueblo where the water cuts down through." (Harrington.)
Location: east side of the Río Grande, just below the point where
the Nambé River enters the Río Grande, about twenty miles
northwest of Santa Fé, New Mexico.
Linguistic group: Tewa.
Period of occupation: since about 1300.
Construction: adobe, plaza type, recent scattering.
Population (1948): 170.
Reservation: 19,844 acres.
Annual *fiesta* and dances: January 23.

According to tradition and the archaeological and historical
records, building has shifted north and south across the plazas
of San Ildefonso for generations. Despite all these shifts, due to
war and internal strife, the plaza pattern has survived. Many of
the rooms making up the central house block dividing the two
plazas no longer serve as living rooms, but are used for storage
or are completely abandoned. The circular kiva in the South
Plaza is typical of the Río Grande area, but a recent innovation

47

San Ildefonso

PLATE VIII

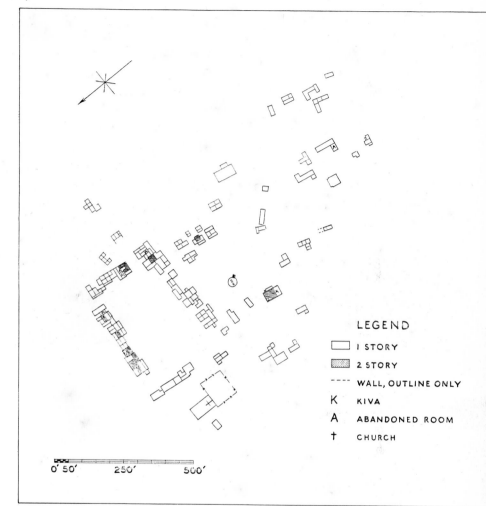

San Ildefonso

FIGURE 10

is the two-story, rectangular kiva located just to the southwest of the old one. A specialized, rectangular room in the two-story structure in the northwest corner of the North Plaza serves as the kiva for that portion of the village. The church, built about 1905, occupies the site of an earlier structure but has no planned relationship to the village.

The work of one potter María Martínez, has made San Ildefonso pottery perhaps the most widely known of all modern pueblo styles. María and her late husband, Julián, developed the popular matte-black design on polished black ware, now made by other potters in the village and also copied, in a cruder form, at Santo Domingo. The later polished wares with deeply carved designs also sell well.

Nambé

From the native name Nambe'e, "pueblo of the mound of earth."
(Harrington.)
Location: north bank of the Nambé River, about sixteen miles
north of Santa Fé, New Mexico.
Linguistic group: Tewa.
Period of occupation: at least since 1300.
Construction: adobe, plaza type.
Population (1948): 155.
Reservation: 18,788 acres.
Annual *fiesta:* October 4.

On the ground, Nambé has the same appearance as any one of
the clusters of Mexican houses up and down the Nambé Valley;
only the circular kiva and the faint outline of old rooms give a
clue to the real nature of the town. From the air, the Indian pattern is obvious, though reduced to a vestige; the largest house
block shows its growth by accretion rather than by plan, an Indian building trait seen in every pueblo. The sherds from the
refuse mounds of this once much larger village indicate a long

Nambé

PLATE IX

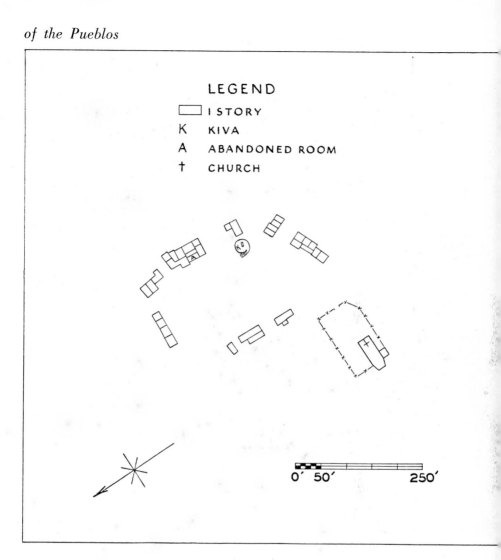

LEGEND
☐ 1 STORY
K KIVA
A ABANDONED ROOM
† CHURCH

0′ 50′ 250′

Nambé

FIGURE 11

period of occupation. Nambé is one of the pueblos that will completely lose its distinguishing characteristics in the not too distant future.

Except for some belt-weaving, introduced by students who learned the technique at the Indian school in Santa Fé, Nambé can be removed from the list of craft-producing villages.

Tesuque

Spanish corruption of the native Tewa name Tatunge, "dry spotted place." (Harrington.)

Location: west bank of the Tesuque River, about ten miles north of Santa Fé, New Mexico.

Linguistic group: Tewa.

Period of occupation: since about 1300.

Construction: adobe, plaza type, recent scattering.

Population (1948): 160.

Reservation: 17,024 acres.

Annual *fiesta* and Harvest Dance: November 12.

Tesuque is an excellent example of the plaza layout in pueblo-building, a pattern often seen in prehistoric ruins (see Fig. 2). Sherds found within the pueblo and on the adjacent mounds indicate that the site has been occupied since about 1300. The present church, built about 1915, is in the same location as an earlier structure, but is fortuitous in its placement and has no relationship to the town plan. Rectangular rooms within the house blocks

55

Tesuque

PLATE X

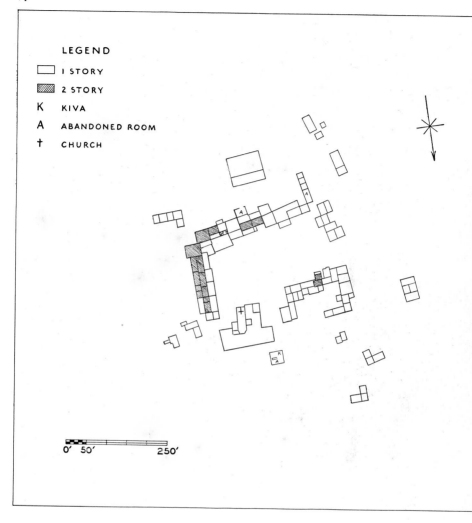

LEGEND
☐ I STORY
▨ 2 STORY
K KIVA
A ABANDONED ROOM
† CHURCH

0′ 50′   250′

Tesuque

FIGURE 12

serve as kivas. An abandoned square kiva stands just to the north-west of the church.

Any pottery object seen in a curio store or Indian market—ash tray, Rain God, small jar or plate—gaudily decorated in pinks, purples, greens, blues, and other rainbow hues, probably came from Tesuque. Older Tesuque pottery was well made and in traditional style. This newer product, decorated with tempera water colors which rub off with the slightest moisture, flourishes and increases because of tourist demand. If the white man will buy it, the Indian will make it. Cochití and Jémez are also beginning to make this type of pottery.

Jémez

From the native word Hemis, meaning "Jémez people." The native name for the village is Walatowa, "the pueblo in the cañon," to distinguish it from the earlier villages farther north. (Harrington.)

Location: east bank of the Jémez River, about twenty miles northwest of Bernalillo, New Mexico.

Linguistic group: Towa.

Period of occupation: probably founded during the latter part of the sixteenth century.

Construction: adobe, modified parallel-street type, recent scattering.

Population (1948): 883.

Reservation: 42,793 acres.

Annual *fiesta* and Harvest Dance: November 12.

The mountain area immediately to the north of Jémez Pueblo contains many ruins of villages formerly occupied by Jémez people, who from all evidence have declined greatly in numbers since the coming of the Spaniards. Many causes have contributed: reprisals by the Spanish, epidemics, raids by the Navajos and Utes, and migration to join other Pueblo groups or the Navajo. Jémez is the last surviving Towa-speaking village. Archaeologi-

Jémez

PLATE XI

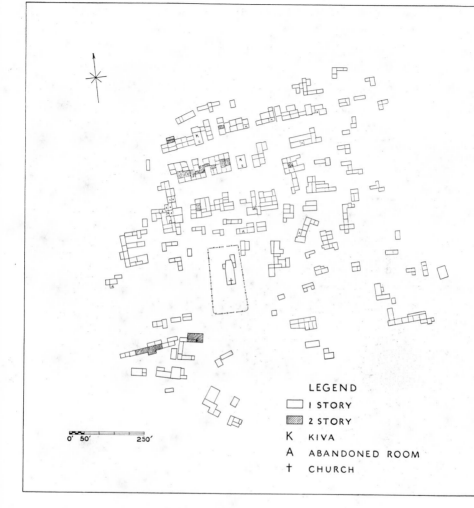

LEGEND

☐ 1 STORY

▨ 2 STORY

K   KIVA

A   ABANDONED ROOM

† CHURCH

0′ 50′   250′

Jémez

FIGURE 13

cally we know very little concerning the founding of Jémez. A mission was built at this site in 1622 and destroyed by fire in 1623; these facts indicate that a town existed here at that date. Sherd evidence of an earlier occupation is lacking. Photographs taken of Jémez in the eighteen eighties show many two-story houses; today most are single story. This flattening out of the buildings is apparent in almost every one of the existing pueblo towns. The pattern of small fields, to the west of the village, is typical of Pueblo agriculture. The kivas at Jémez are large rectangular structures, one separate, the other built into a house group.

Large wickerwork baskets woven of willow twigs, and the twilled ringbaskets of yucca leaves, have long been the best-known Jémez products. Some weaving and embroidery work on cotton cloth are also done.

Cochití

From the native name. (Harrington.)
Location: west bank of the Río Grande, about thirty miles south-
west of Santa Fé, New Mexico.
Linguistic group: Keresan.
Period of occupation: Sherds found in the refuse mounds show
a continuous series from at least 1250 to the present.
Construction: adobe, plaza type, recent scattering.
Population (1948): 497.
Reservation: 22,763 acres.
Annual *fiesta* and Corn Dance: July 14.

Cochití, most northern of the Keresan groups, shows very clearly
the breakup of the old village system. The plaza still serves as
the central features of communal life, but the newer houses are
built at a distance from it, and the original compact pattern
is being lost. Two circular kivas are located outside the plaza.
The sandy point of the hills overlooking the bottom lands of
the Río Grande has been occupied for at least 700 years. Old
foundation stones and old-type wall construction can be seen in

63

Cochití

PLATE XII

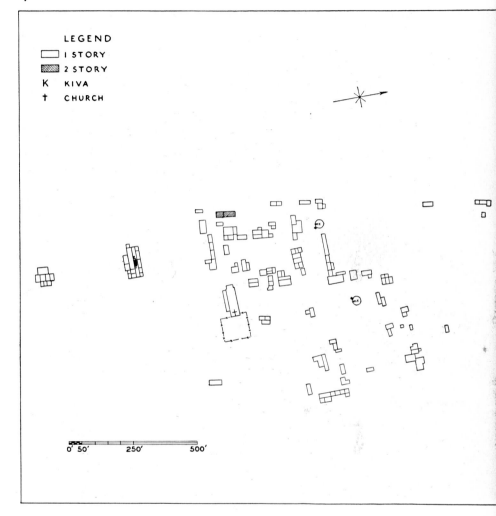

LEGEND
☐ I STORY
▨ 2 STORY
K KIVA
† CHURCH

0' 50'   250'   500'

Cochití

FIGURE 14

many sections of the town, and sherds of prehistoric types are abundant in the refuse mounds—all evidence of long occupation.

Pottery of Cochití is characterized by black designs on a warm, pinkish, cream-colored slip. The designs often occur as individual units rather than in connected bands; graphic representations are more apt to be used here than on the pottery of any of the other Río Grande villages. Cochití is perhaps most famous for its drums made out of hollowed cottonwood logs.

Santo Domingo

Spanish for St. Dominic. The native name is Kiua. (Harrington.)

Location: east bank of the Río Grande, about thirty miles southwest of Santa Fé, New Mexico.

Linguistic group: Keresan.

Period of occupation: The major portion of the present pueblo has been built since 1886, at which time a large part of the old village was washed away by floods. Photographs taken in 1880 show that the street layout was the same as now. This site is known to have been occupied by Santo Domingans since about 1700, although possibly an earlier site exists at this location.

Construction: adobe, parallel-street type.

Population (1948): 1,106.

Reservation: 66,231 acres.

Annual *fiesta* and Green Corn Dance: August 4.

Lummis, in his *Mesa, Cañon and Pueblo*, refers to this town as "Santo Domingo, stiffest necked of the pueblos in clinging to the ways of the old." This statement still holds, and visitors and innovations are not welcome. The conservative nature of the inhabitants is very apparent in looking at the aerial view of the village; all house-building is confined to the immediate area, and there is none of the trend seen in other pueblos for individual homes to be built in the fields or open spaces surrounding the pueblo.

67

Santo Domingo

PLATE XIII

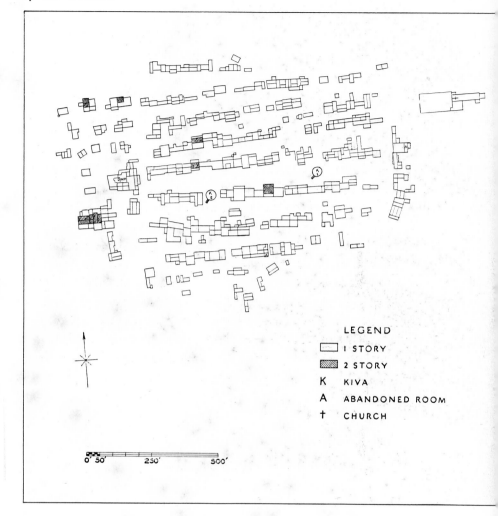

LEGEND

◻ 1 STORY

▨ 2 STORY

K KIVA

A ABANDONED ROOM

† CHURCH

0' 50'   250'   500'

Santo Domingo

FIGURE 15

Santo Domingo

Here each individual lives with the group and is closely controlled by tradition. The layout of the village is in long house blocks along parallel streets. This same pattern can also be seen in Acoma and Old Oraibi, and to a lesser extent in Jémez, Santa Ana, and San Juan. It is a pattern which, though less common than the plaza type, is definitely prehistoric. The wider central "street" serves as the space where dances are held. There are two circular kivas, one in the central street, the other between house blocks. The church is situated outside the village proper and has no relationship to the ground plan.

Santo Domingo pottery, like the people of the pueblo, is bold in execution and conservative in design innovations. Geometric patterns in black on a cream-colored slip characterize the dominant ware, though a crude imitation of the San Ildefonso black type is now being made in large amounts. There is some silverwork, but more manufacture of turquoise and shell beads. Santo Domingo claims the turquoise deposits at Los Cerrillos. The white man's plastics—old combs, phonograph records, and toothbrushes—are often employed by Santo Domingan artisans to produce necklaces and other ornaments.

San Felipe

Spanish for St. Philip. The native name is Katishtya. (Harrington.)

Location: west bank of the Río Grande, about thirty miles north of Albuquerque, New Mexico.

Linguistic group: Keresan.

Period of occupation: The present pueblo was built sometime during the first part of the eighteenth century.

Construction: adobe, plaza type, some recent scattering.

Population (1948): 784.

Reservation: 43,201 acres.

Annual *fiesta* and Green Corn Dance: May 1.

San Felipe, like its neighbor to the north, Santo Domingo, must be included among the most conservative of the present pueblo groups. The main portion of the village is laid out around the central plaza, but there is more building away from this central location than at Santo Domingo, some of the houses being located on the east bank of the river. The plaza, is unusual in that it is sunken; the main portion is at least three feet below the ground

San Felipe

PLATE XIV

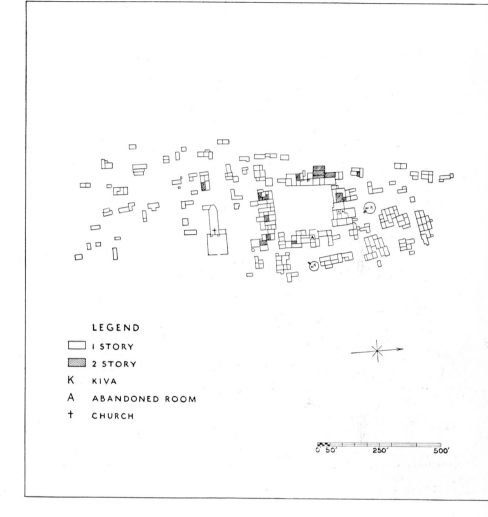

LEGEND
☐ 1 STORY
▨ 2 STORY
K KIVA
A ABANDONED ROOM
† CHURCH

0′ 50′ 250′ 500′

San Felipe

FIGURE 16

San Felipe

level of the surrounding houses, affording a bowl setting for the colorful dances. The circular kivas are situated outside the main plaza.

No pottery has been made at San Felipe since about 1700, and other handcrafts are equally lacking.

Santa Ana

Spanish for St. Anne. The native name is Tamaja. (Harrington.)
Location: north bank of the Jémez River, about eight miles north-
west of Bernalillo, New Mexico.
Linguistic group: Keresan.
Period of occupation: probably founded about 1700.
Construction: irregular-stone masonry and adobe, parallel-street
type, modified.
Population (1948): 288.
Reservation: 19,136 acres.
Annual *fiesta* and Green Corn Dance: July 26.

Santa Ana, like Zía farther upstream, occupies a barren location facing the sandy bed of the Jémez River. Since farm land
and water are at a minimum here, most of the people have moved
to reservation land along the Río Grande, where the settlements
known as the Ranchos de Santa Ana have grown up. These new
villages have the same appearance as the small Mexican settlements along the valley; they are European in their layout, but
definitely are not an amalgamation of racial groups, merely a

Santa Ana

PLATE XV

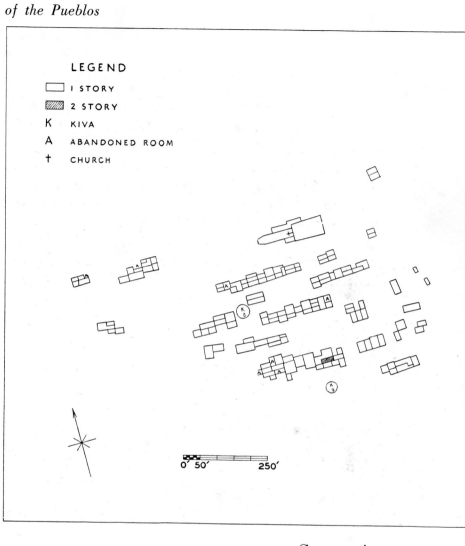

LEGEND
☐ 1 STORY
▨ 2 STORY
K KIVA
A ABANDONED ROOM
† CHURCH

0' 50'   250'

Santa Ana

FIGURE 17

borrowing of town pattern. Visits are made to the old village for various ceremonies and dances; a few people remain there to watch the village and prevent unwanted intrusions. Sherd evidence indicates that Santa Ana was not occupied until after the Reconquest; the location of the older town bearing the same name is unknown. The parallel-street arrangement is somewhat modified into plazas. Two circular kivas are present.

Distinctive pottery was produced for many years in this village, and recently an attempt has been made to revive the craft after a period of years when none was made. The brick-red pottery was finished with a thin white slip and decorated with red and black designs; unlike conventional practice in most pueblo pottery design, the red areas were often not outlined with black.

Zía

From the native name Tseja. (Harrington.)
Location: north bank of the Jémez River, about sixteen miles
   northwest of Bernalillo, New Mexico.
Linguistic group: Keresan.
Period of occupation: since about 1300.
Construction: irregular stone masonry and adobe, plaza type.
Population (1948): 267.
Reservation: 16,669 acres.
Annual *fiesta* and Green Corn Dance: August 15.

Zía, situated on a location lacking sufficient farm land and water, has remained a small, compact pueblo, retaining to a marked
degree the typical prehistoric plaza pattern. However, internal
strife marks Zía communal life. The circular kiva nearest the
river was burned by a rival faction within the pueblo the day
before the Corn Dance in 1947 and has not been rebuilt. Corrals
for the livestock, always present in the pueblos, are especially
prominent on Zía's barren site. Unlike Santa Ana, the people of

Zía

PLATE XVI

LEGEND

☐ I STORY

---- WALL, OUTLINE ONLY

K KIVA

A ABANDONED ROOM

† CHURCH

0' 50' 250'

Zía

FIGURE 18

Zía

Zía do not have any reservation land along the Río Grande to which they can move for better farming conditions, and thus the future of the group is limited.

The inhabitants of Zía have long been held almost as social outcasts by other Pueblo people, all of whom, however, have been willing to trade for and use the well-made pottery produced at Zía. Oftentimes, the pottery traded to Jémez has brought in the food needed to help the people through the years when their poor farm land did not produce enough for subsistence. The pottery has the same color combinations as that from Santa Ana, but is much better made, with more skillful line work and greater variety of design. Zía pottery can always be distinguished from that made at Acoma or Santa Ana by the tiny black inclusions—ground-up bits of basalt or lava—found in the clay making up the body of the vessel.

Laguna

Spanish for "lagoon" or "lake"; so called on account of a large pond west of the pueblo. The native name is Ka-waik'. (Hodge.)
Location: north bank of the Río San José, about forty-five miles west of Albuquerque, New Mexico.
Linguistic group: Keresan.
Period of occupation: founded in 1699.
Construction: stone masonry and adobe, plaza type, recent scattering.
Population (1948): 2,894.
Reservation: 249,396 acres.
Annual *fiesta* and Harvest Dance: September 19.

Although listed as the largest of all the pueblos, Laguna itself is not very extensive in the original layout. The plan and photograph do not give a truly accurate picture of the location of the village. It lies on a rounded, rocky point above the river; the houses nearer the curved roadway are much below the level of those surrounding the plaza, and the visual impression of terraced houses is due to their being built up along the rather steep slope of the hill. Photographs taken in 1887 show that there were

83

Laguna

PLATE XVII

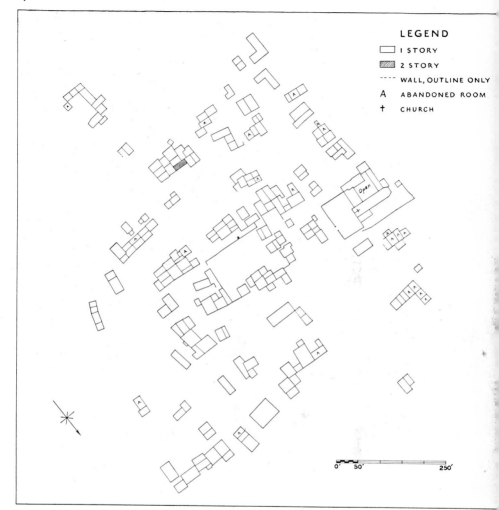

Laguna

FIGURE 19

three-story houses around the plaza and that the plaza was more completely enclosed than it is now. The oldest part of the town is that immediately surrounding the plaza and the section just to the south. The church, built in 1700, is outside the main area. According to Parsons, the absence of kivas in Laguna is due to the removal of the conservative, religious group to Mesita and Isleta, about 1880, leaving the nonreligious, "Americanized" group in control. What may be considered greater Laguna takes in the old central village and the suburbs of Paraje, Paguate, Encinal, Casa Blanca, Mesita Negra, and Seama with its three satellites (New York, Philadelphia, and Harrisburg), situated at varying distances from old Laguna.

Some pottery has been made at Laguna, but it is practically indistinguishable from Acoma pottery. Some of the finest examples of Pueblo embroidery have come from Laguna and Acoma, but this is now a vanishing art, the newer specimens being far inferior to the old pieces.

Acoma

From the native name Akóme, "people of the white rock." Their
name for the town is A'ko. (Hodge.)

Location: some sixty miles west of Albuquerque, New Mexico,
and about ten miles south of the Río San José.

Linguistic group: Keresan.

Period of occupation: From sherds found at Acoma it is evident
that this site has been occupied for at least one thousand
years.

Construction: stone masonry, parallel-street type.

Population (1948): 1,447.

Reservation: 153,844 acres.

Annual *fiesta* and Harvest Dance: September 2.

Acoma, which contends with Oraibi for the title of oldest continuously occupied town in the United States, is considered one
of the most spectacular pueblos. Situated on a high, isolated
sandstone mesa, it is an outstanding example of a defensive location. The majority of the population now live in secondary
villages, McCarty's and Acomita, near the farm lands along the
San José and return to the old town only at the times of the various dances. Part of the town was burned by the Spanish in 1559,

Acoma

PLATE XVIII

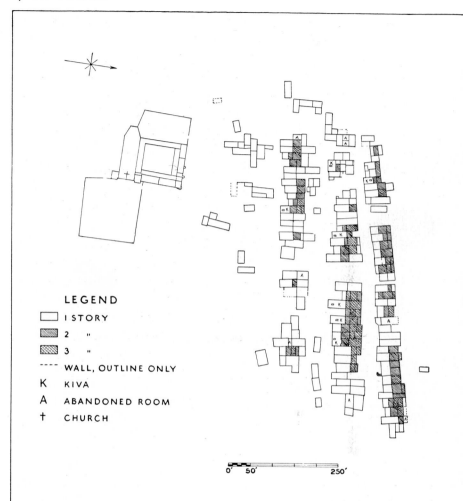

LEGEND

☐ I STORY

▨ 2 "

▨ 3 "

- - - WALL, OUTLINE ONLY

K KIVA

A ABANDONED ROOM

† CHURCH

0' 50'   250'

Acoma

FIGURE 20

but the present buildings undoubtedly follow the aboriginal pattern of terraced house blocks in parallel lines. The great stone and adobe mission church, built prior to 1644, has undergone burnings and numerous repairs. Since there is no soil on the rocky surface of the mesa, all the earth used to build the pueblo and the church and to fill the churchyard had to be carried up from the valley below. The kivas at Acoma, seven in number, are rectangular and form an integral part of the house blocks in which they are situated. The water supply of the town is dependent on small catchment basins in the rock. Three of these can be seen in the aerial view, the one at the east end of the house blocks being most conspicuous.

For generations, Acoma has made great quantities of fine, thin pottery, distinctive with its white slip and designs in dark brown or black, reds, yellows, tans, or orange. The designs range from geometric to involved curvilinear patterns, often featuring the parrot. Nowadays, most of the pieces made are small and serve no utilitarian purpose other than curio sale.

Zuñi

According to Hodge, a Spanish adaptation of the Keresan name
   Sunyítsi. The Zuñi tribal name is A'shiwi.
Location: western New Mexico, about forty miles south of Gallup.
Linguistic group: Zuñian.
Period of occupation: major portion of the present village built
   after 1693.
Construction: stone masonry, plaza type, recent scattering.
Population (1948): 2,671.
Reservation: 343,743 acres.
Shalako ceremony: late November or early December.

The present village of Zuñi occupies the site of the old pueblo
of Halona, one of the towns visited by Coronado in 1540. Halona
fell into decay during the Pueblo Revolt, but after the Reconquest the pueblo was rebuilt and all the Zuñi Indians were con-
centrated there. The now abandoned church probably occupies
the same location and possibly consists in part of the same walls
as the building of 1666; the mission was burned in 1680 and
rebuilt in 1699. At one time the terraced houses of Zuñi rose to
a height of five stories around the plazas, but now, for the most
part, they are reduced to a single story. The town still retains
the appearance of height, however, for the houses are built on

Zuñi

PLATE XIX

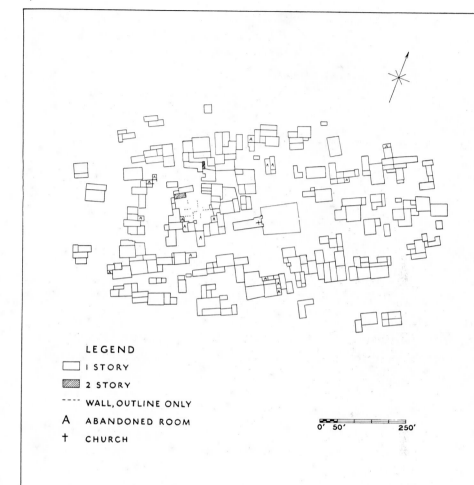

LEGEND

☐ I STORY

▨ 2 STORY

---- WALL, OUTLINE ONLY

A ABANDONED ROOM

† CHURCH

0' 50'   250'

Zuñi

FIGURE 21

the mounds of the older dwellings. Most of the new houses are of cutstone masonry of good quality; the older sections show the cruder work of earlier times. The ground plan of Zuñi (Fig. 21) is based on the old section of the town, north of the Zuñi River and south of the road running east and west. The extended portions of the town, which have grown up largely since 1900, consist of some compact house blocks and many individual homes. Most of these new buildings are of cut-stone construction. The stone-walled garden plots, so distinctive of this pueblo, show in the aerial photograph to the west and to the southeast of the old section. The population figure given includes Zuñi proper and the permanent farming villages of Pescado, Nutria, Ojo Caliente, and Tekapo.

Now almost a lost art in the pueblo, pottery-making here once reached a high degree of perfection. Chalky-white slip with sharply contrasting designs of red and black were the characteristic features of this ware. Metal and stone work, principally in silver and turquoise, has replaced this traditional craft. One can almost say that Zuñi is a single-guild town, with hundreds of the people turning out fine silver and turquoise ornaments. Many of the workers have the latest models of jewelers' stone-cutting machines and power tools to assist them in their work. At present a large percentage of Indian jewelry sold in shops all over the country is made at Zuñi. An interesting sidelight on the rapidly disappearing potter's craft is illustrated by a recent incident. About 1930, a trader at Zuñi sold a curio dealer in Santa Fé a large lot of modern Zuñi pottery. After World War II, this same trader opened a new store in Gallup; and wishing to display a large selection of Zuñi wares, he attempted to purchase pottery in the village, but none was obtainable. In the meantime, the Santa Fé dealer had gone out of business and stored his stock in a warehouse. This pottery, now back in Gallup, was the only large collection outside of museums to bear witness of the once flourishing ceramic art of Zuñi.

Walpi

From the native words *wala*, "gap" or "notch," and *ovi*, "place"
—"place of the notch," in reference to the gap in the mesa
to the northeast of Hano. (Colton and Baxter.)
Location: on the tip of First Mesa, or the easternmost of the three
Hopi mesas, fingerlike projections from the southern edge
of Black Mesa, about seventy miles north of Winslow,
Arizona.
Linguistic group: Shoshonean.
Period of occupation: founded shortly after 1680.
Construction: stone masonry, extended house groups.
Population (1932): 163.
Reservation: 2,472,320 acres (total acreage for the Hopi Res-
ervation).
Snake Dance: August of odd-numbered years.

The narrow mesa location of Walpi has largely determined the
layout of the village. Since the mesa, at its greatest width, is
barely 150 feet across, there is no room for large courts or plazas.
As is true with all the older Hopi towns, a comparison with Mindeleff's plans made in 1882 will show a decided change, especially in the number of rooms and the height of buildings; the
basic pattern remains, but the outlines are becoming blurred.
The older towns are being abandoned in favor of the more acces-

Walpi

PLATE XX

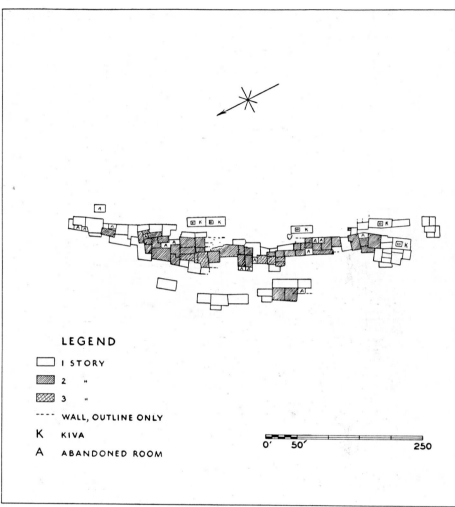

LEGEND

☐ I STORY

▨ 2 "

▨ 3 "

---- WALL, OUTLINE ONLY

K KIVA

A ABANDONED ROOM

0' 50'   250

Walpi

FIGURE 22

sible locations at the foot of the mesas, or scattered individual homes. Five rectangular kivas are present. An innovation, doubtless borrowed from the white man, can be seen along the edge of the mesa on the east side—a guard fence to keep children and the visitors to the dances from falling over the cliff. The present village was built after the Pueblo Revolt; the older site was located on the lower terrace, just below the tip of the mesa.

Hano

Also called Tewa. According to Colton and Baxter, *Hano* is said
to be a nickname given by the Hopi because the Tewa inhabitants say "Ha" every other word. But it is more likely
derived from Los Tanos, the name by which eighteenth
century manuscripts refer to the Tanoan-speaking Indians,
some of whom moved to the Hopi country after the Pueblo
Revolt.

Location: on the First Mesa, the first group of houses on the road
leading up from Polacca. See Walpi.

Linguistic group: Tewa.

Period of occupation: founded about 1700.

Construction: stone masonry, plaza type.

Population (1932): 309.

Reservation: See Walpi.

Hano was built by Tewa Indians from the Río Grande area who
moved to the Hopi country after the Pueblo Revolt. According
to custom, such outside groups were not allowed to settle on Hopi
land unless they could provide some definite service to the Hopi
town which controlled the desired location. The Tewa were given
the task of defending the trail leading up to Walpi; here on the
strategic spot at the top of the trail they built their village. The
town has a plaza layout and the general appearance of other Hopi

towns. The rectangular kiva has been adopted from the Hopi, and by all indications Hano is a Hopi village in everything except language. The dividing line between Hano and Sichomovi is not apparent to a visitor on First Mesa, the houses forming a continuous string along the narrow mesa top; the division used in the ground plan (Fig. 23) is based on Mindeleff's drawings.

Pottery-making in the Hopi towns is confined largely to those of First Mesa, especially Hano. The craft degenerated from prehistoric times until the eighteen nineties, when a Hano potter, Nampeyo, seeing some of the fine old pieces being excavated from near-by ruins, began a revival of the art. Hopi pottery is characterized by its hardness, its cream or tan color, and its designs in dark brown and reddish brown.

Sichomovi

"Place of the mound where wild currant bushes grow." (Colton
and Baxter.)
Location: on First Mesa, between Hano and Walpi. See Walpi.
Linguistic group: Shoshonean.
Period of occupation: founded about 1750.
Construction: stone masonry, plaza type.
Population (1932): 315.
Reservation: See Walpi.

The narrowness of the mesa top has dictated to a large degree
the growth and plan of all three villages on First Mesa. In
Sichomovi, as in Hano, the central plaza is small, and long house
blocks run parallel to the edge of the cliff. Sichomovi was built
in the mid-eighteenth century by a group from Walpi together
with a few Indians from the Río Grande region. The long, black-
roofed building on the west side of the mesa and toward the
boundary line of Hano is at present occupied by a Protestant

Hano, LOWER LEFT

Sichomovi, UPPER RIGHT

PLATE XXI

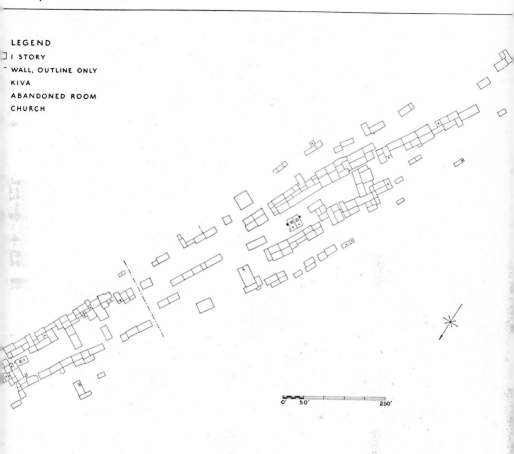

LEGEND
I STORY
WALL, OUTLINE ONLY
KIVA
ABANDONED ROOM
CHURCH

0'   50'   250'

LOWER LEFT, **Hano**

UPPER RIGHT, **Sichomovi**

FIGURE 23

103

church. Unlike the Río Grande pueblo people, the Hopi have consistently resisted Catholic missionary influence since 1680. Protestant efforts have been a little more successful.

A great deal of pottery, similar to that made in Hano, is produced here for commercial sale.

Mishongnovi

"Place of the black man," in reference to the Crow Clan. (Colton and Baxter.)
Location: on Second Mesa. See Walpi.
Linguistic group: Shoshonean.
Period of occupation: founded about 1700.
Construction: stone masonry, plaza type, recent scattering.
Population (1932): 266.
Reservation: See Walpi.
Snake Dance: August of odd-numbered years.

The houses of Mishongnovi cover almost completely the available space on the mesa top, conforming to all the irregularities of the surface and the confining outline of the rocky finger. A tradition among the Hopi regarding the founding of Mishongnovi on its original site gives further insight into the feuds always present between Pueblo people, even when living close together and of the same linguistic group. The story goes that at one time people of the Crow Clan came from the region of the San Fran-

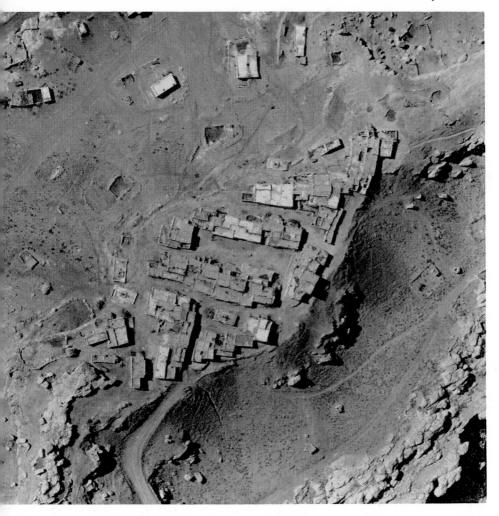

Mishongnovi

PLATE XXII

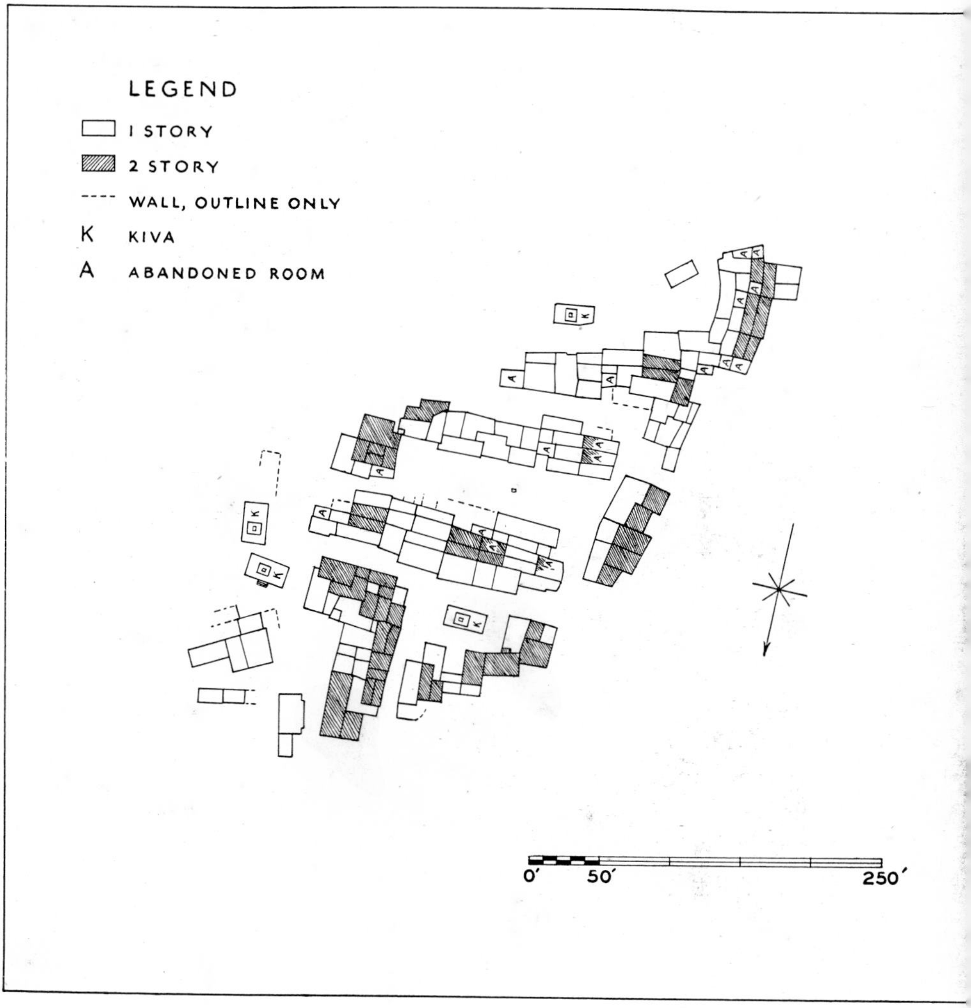

LEGEND

☐ I STORY

▨ 2 STORY

---- WALL, OUTLINE ONLY

K KIVA

A ABANDONED ROOM

0' 50' 250'

Mishongnovi

FIGURE 24

cisco Mountains and asked permission from the people of Shongopovi to settle near them. Permission was finally granted for them
to build by the Corn Rock, a Shongopovi shrine, on condition
that they protect it from the people of Walpi. The present location was occupied after the Pueblo Revolt.

Craftwork of the Second Mesa Hopi towns is featured by
the specialization in coiled basketry in the shape of plaques,
trays, and deep baskets.

Shipaulovi

"The mosquitoes," from the tradition that the people came from
a village near Winslow, Arizona, which they were forced
to leave because of the hordes of mosquitoes along the Little
Colorado River. (Colton and Baxter.)
Location: on Second Mesa. See Walpi.
Linguistic group: Shoshonean.
Period of occupation: founded about 1700.
Construction: stone masonry, plaza type.
Population (1932): 123.
Reservation: See Walpi.

Shipaulovi, the smallest of the Hopi towns, still has the same
compact appearance of all those situated on the limiting confines
of a small mesa. The location and house arrangement around a
plaza are of defensive value. Another characteristic of Hopi
town-planning is the covered passageways leading into the plazas.
The ground plan of Shipaulovi is surprisingly like that of
Homolobi No. 2 (Fig. 3), a prehistoric pueblo located on the
Little Colorado River near Winslow, Arizona. A feature of most

Shipaulovi

PLATE XXIII

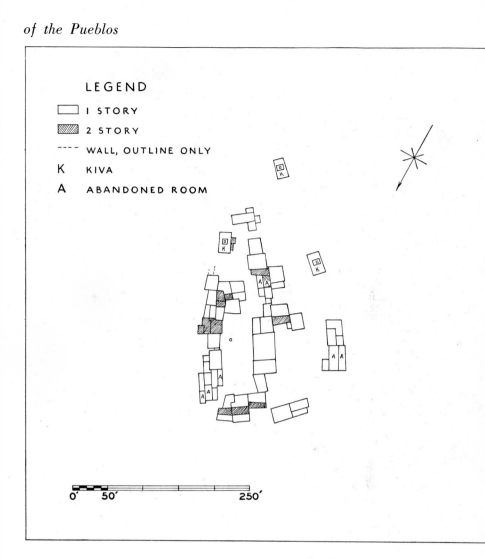

LEGEND

☐ I STORY

▨ 2 STORY

---- WALL, OUTLINE ONLY

K KIVA

A ABANDONED ROOM

0′ 50′   250′

Shipaulovi

FIGURE 25

Shipaulovi

of the old Hopi towns is the small shrine usually found in the plaza, a boxlike structure of stone and adobe, about two feet square, in which are placed prayer plumes and offerings. The aerial view clearly shows the shrine in the upper left-hand portion of the inner plaza.

Of all the craft products of the Hopi, perhaps none are better known than the Kachina dolls. Among the Pueblo Indians, Kachinas are sacred, supernatural personages or beings of the elaborate Indian pantheon, and are impersonated in ceremonies by masked dancers. The term *Kachina* is also applied to the masked dancers and the miniature effigies which are made for the ceremony. Commercialization has touched the Kachinas, so that now hundreds of these gaily decorated little effigies, or "dolls," are made for sale with no thought of their religious significance. All the Hopi towns are represented in this craft.

Shongopovi

"Place by the spring where the tall reeds grow." (Colton and
 Baxter.)
Location: on Second Mesa. See Walpi.
Linguistic group: Shoshonean.
Period of occupation: founded about 1680.
Construction: stone masonry, plaza type, recent scattering.
Population (1932): 307.
Reservation: See Walpi.
Snake Dance: August of even-numbered years.

Like all other Hopi mesa towns herein presented, with the ex-
ception of Old Oraibi, Shongopovi was built after 1680, when
the people moved to more easily defended locations in fear of
reprisals from the Spanish; there was also increasing pressure
from the Utes and Navajos. In all Pueblo towns, there is a constant minor change in the layout and relationship of buildings.
The aerial view of Shongopovi shows a gap between the houses
in the long central house block, but when the site was visited after

113

Shongopovi

PLATE XXIV

114

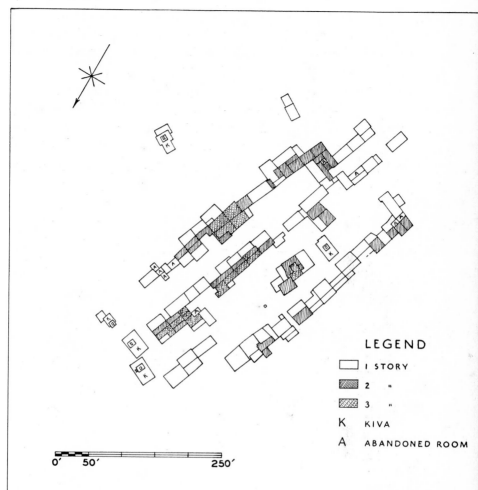

LEGEND

☐ I STORY

▨ 2 "

▨ 3 "

K KIVA

A ABANDONED ROOM

0' 50' 250'

Shongopovi

FIGURE 26

the photograph was taken, a new house was being built to connect across this gap. Again it must be stated that the plans for each village are of the present, immediate date, and will not apply in all details ten years from now.

Many of the baskets, both the coiled type made on Second Mesa and the wickerwork baskets of Third Mesa, bear designs representing different Kachina masks. Formerly the designs were worked in with the available natural-colored vegetal materials or colored with native dyes, now almost all the colors come from aniline sources.

Oraibi

"The place of the rock called Orai." (Colton and Baxter.)
Location: on Third Mesa. See Walpi.
Linguistic group: Shoshonean.
Period of occupation: since about 1150.
Construction: stone masonry, parallel-street type.
Population (1932): 87.
Reservation: See Walpi.

Once the largest and most important of the Hopi towns, Oraibi has declined rapidly since 1906, when an administrative dispute developed and many of the people moved away to found Hotevilla. More and more of the inhabitants are moving down to New Oraibi. In many instances they literally take their houses with them, using the stone from the old walls with which to rebuild, and thus hastening the rapid disintegration of the old town. A

Oraibi

PLATE XXV

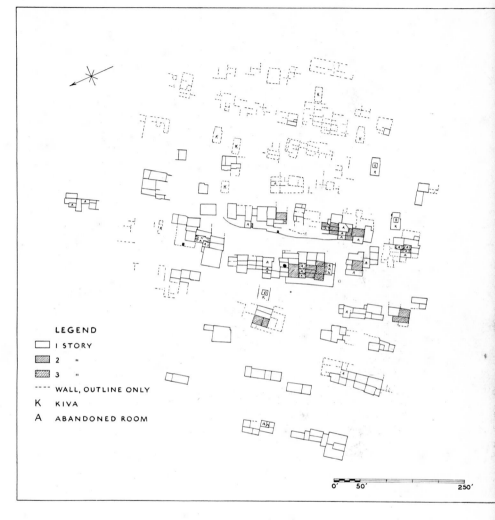

LEGEND

☐ I STORY

▨ 2 "

▨ 3 "

---- WALL, OUTLINE ONLY

K KIVA

A ABANDONED ROOM

0' 50'   250'

Oraibi

FIGURE 27

mission was built here in 1629 but now shows only as a low mound north of the village.

Only by archaeological excavation in the refuse mounds of Acoma and Old Oraibi can the claim to the title of oldest continuously occupied town in the United States be settled. Both are old, and Oraibi, fast becoming archaeology before our eyes, gives added evidence of the need to preserve a record of all the pueblos as they look today. They are all changing, and more and more of them will become archaeology as time goes on. The roofless rooms in many of the house blocks shown in the lower half of the aerial view of Oraibi portend the eventual condition seen in the upper area, in which bare outlines of rooms sketch a pattern on the mounds of fallen houses.

Bibliography

Aberle, S. D. *The Pueblo Indians of New Mexico; Their Land, Economy and Civil Organization. Memoir No. 70*, American Anthropological Association. Menasha, Wisconsin, 1948.

Bandelier, Adolf F. *Investigations Among the Indians of the Southwestern United States*. Final *Report*, Parts I and II. Cambridge, Massachusetts, 1890, 1892.

Brew, John Otis. *Archaeology of Alkali Ridge, Southeastern Utah. Papers* of the Peabody Museum of American Archaeology and Ethnology, Vol. XXI. Cambridge, Massachusetts, 1946.

Colton, Harold S., and Frank C. Baxter. *Days in the Painted Desert and the San Francisco Mountains*. Museum of Northern Arizona. Flagstaff, Arizona, 1932.

——and L. L. Hargrave. *Handbook of Northern Arizona Pottery Wares*. Museum of Northern Arizona *Bulletin No. 4*. Flagstaff, Arizona, 1937.

Harrington, John P. *The Ethnogeography of the Tewa Indians*. Twenty-ninth *Annual Report* of the Bureau of American Ethnology. Washington, 1916.

Hodge, Frederick Webb (ed.) *Handbook of American Indians. Bulletin 30*, Parts 1 and 2, Bureau of American Ethnology. Washington, 1910.

Kidder, Alfred Vincent. *Introduction to the Study of Southwestern Archaeology. Papers*, Southwestern Expedition, Phillips Academy. New Haven, Connecticut, 1924.

——and Anna O. Shepard. *The Pottery of Pecos*. Vol. 2. *Papers*, Southwestern Expedition, Phillips Academy. New Haven, Connecticut, 1936.

Kubler, George. *Mexican Architecture in the Sixteenth Century*. New Haven, Connecticut, Yale University Press, 1948.

121

————. *The Religious Architecture of New Mexico. Contributions* of the Taylor Museum of the Colorado Springs Fine Arts Center. Colorado Springs, Colorado, Taylor Museum, 1940. Printed by Yale University Press.

Linton, Ralph. "Nomad Raids and Fortified Pueblos," *American Antiquity*, Vol. X, No. 1 (July, 1944), 28–32.

McGregor, John C. *Southwestern Archaeology.* New York, John Wiley and Sons, 1941.

Mera, H. P. *A Survey of the Biscuit Ware Area in Northern New Mexico.* Laboratory of Anthropology, Technical Series, *Bulletin No.6.* Santa Fé, New Mexico, 1934.

————. *Ceramic Clues to the Prehistory of North Central New Mexico.* Laboratory of Anthropology, Technical Series, *Bulletin No. 8.* Santa Fé, New Mexico, 1935.

————. *Population Changes in the Rio Grande Glaze-Paint Area.* Laboratory of Anthropology, Technical Series, *Bulletin No. 9.* Santa Fé, New Mexico, 1940.

Mindeleff, Victor. *A Study of Pueblo Architecture: Tusayan and Cibola.* Eighth *Annual Report* of the Bureau of American Ethnology. Washington, 1891.

Reiter, Paul. *The Jémez Pueblo of Unshagi, New Mexico.* Monographs Nos. 5 and 6, School of American Research. Albuquerque, New Mexico, University of New Mexico Press, 1938.

Roberts, Frank H. H. "A Survey of Southwestern Archaeology," *American Anthropologist,* n.s. Vol. XXXVII, No. 1 (January–March, 1935), 1–35.

Stallings, W. S. "Southwestern Dated Ruins: I," *Tree-Ring Bulletin,* Vol. IV, No. 2 (October, 1937), 3–5.

————. *Dating Prehistoric Ruins by Tree Rings.* Laboratory of Anthropology, General Series, *Bulletin No. 8.* Santa Fé, New Mexico, 1939.

U. S. Department of the Interior, National Park Service, Branch of Plans and Design. *Historic American Buildings Survey.* Washington, 1934.

Wormington, H. M. *Prehistoric Indians of the Southwest.* The Colorado Museum of Natural History, Popular Series, No. 7, Denver, Colorado, 1947.

More extensive bibliographies can be found in each of the publications cited.